Where's The
Baby?

Written by Melissa Doodt
Photography by Michael Curtain

sundance™

"Where's the baby?" called Mom.

"She's in the bedroom," said Nina.
"Toys are everywhere."

"Oh no! Not again," said Mom.

3

"Where's the baby?" called Dad.

"She's in the kitchen," said Nina. "Pots are everywhere."

"Oh no! Not again," said Dad.

"Where's the baby?" called Mom.

"She's in the laundry room,"
said Nina.
"Clothes are everywhere."

"Oh no! Not again," said Mom.

7

"Where's the baby?" called Dad.

"She's in the living room,"
said Nina.
"Papers are everywhere."

"Oh no! Not again," said Dad.

"Where's the baby?" called Mom.

"She's in the sandbox," said Nina. "Sand is everywhere."

"Oh no! Not again," said Mom.

"Where's the baby?" called Dad.

"She's in the bathroom," said Nina
"Powder is everywhere."

"Oh no! Not again," said Dad.

"Where's the baby?" called Mom.

"She's in her crib," said Nina.
"I think she'll go to sleep."